What Is a
Teacher?

To Doug and Scott,
who have taught me so much
—B.L.

To Lili and William
—C.K.

Published by The Millbrook Press, Inc.
2 Old New Milford Road
Brookfield, CT   06804
www.millbrookpress.com

Text copyright © 2000 by Barbara Lehn
Photographs copyright © 2000 by Carol Krauss
Printed in the United States of America

1   3   5   4   2

Library of Congress Cataloging-in-Publication Data
Lehn, Barbara.
What is a teacher? / Barbara Lehn; photographs by Carol Krauss.
p. cm.
Summary: Simple text and photographs depict people engaged in activities
that embody the qualities of a teacher.
ISBN 0-7613-1713-9 (lib. bdg.)
1. Teachers—Juvenile literature. 2. Teachers—Pictorial works—Juvenile
literature. 3. Teaching—Vocational guidance—Juvenile literature.
[1. Teachers. 2. Occupations.] I. Krauss, Carol, ill.
II. Title.
LB1775.L38 2000
371.1—dc21   00-021495

What Is a Teacher?

Barbara Lehn
Photographs by Carol Krauss

The Millbrook Press
Brookfield, Connecticut

A teacher **shares** what she knows.

Hannah teaches Adam how to swing.

"When your feet are in front, lean back. Then put your feet behind you and lean forward, like I do," says Hannah.

A teacher explains **clearly**.

Lili teaches William the difference between "M" and "W."

"The letter 'W' starts at the top, and the 'M' starts at the bottom, like you're making a mountain," explains Lili.

A teacher **coaches** and **guides** practice.

Arya demonstrates how to kick the soccer ball so Sean can practice his passing.

"Try to kick the ball with the inside of your foot, like this," coaches Arya.

A teacher **answers** questions.

Kate, Cole, Michelle, and Victoria are using counters to figure out a math question.

Bryan shows them, "If you keep on trading each blue chip for two yellows, you'd get eight yellows altogether. So, the answer is eight."

A teacher
knows
how to find
answers to
questions.

Jazz and Desiree want to find out where bats live.

Jazz tells Desiree, "We should look under 'B' to find 'bats' and then read the number. That will tell us what page to look on."

A teacher
uses
all kinds of
materials.

Ben and Gabrielle need a bridge to finish their fort.

"If we use these little sticks first," Ben says, "we can put big sticks on top."

A teacher **demonstrates** how to do things.

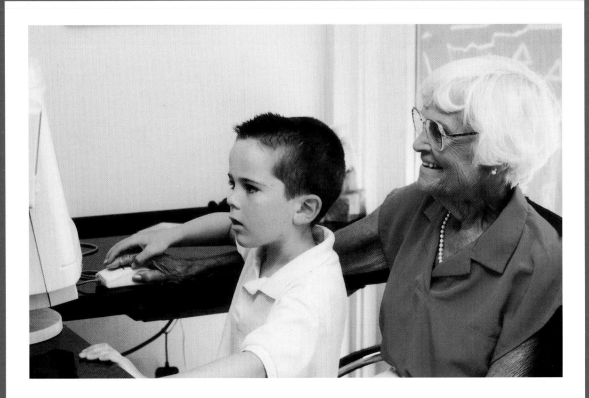

Henry teaches his great-grandmother how to send e-mail.

Henry explains, "After you finish writing your message, you click on this little picture to send your mail."

A teacher is **patient**.

Stewart teaches Seth a boogie-woogie song on the piano.

"Try that again with this finger so you can go back to C," says Stewart.

A teacher is **encouraging**.

Hailey helps Takahiro learn to read.

"'Train' sounds just like 'rain' with a 'T,'" explains Hailey.

A teacher **never gives up**. If one way doesn't work, she tries another.

Rachel tries to teach her dog, Stella, to sit and wait.

"I tried asking her to sit and wait until I said to get the tennis ball, but it didn't work. This time I'll try using a dog biscuit," Rachel thinks.

A teacher makes learning **fun** and **interesting**.

Zac taught his classmates and teacher how to fold a 3-D origami ball.

"Hooray! We did it!" shouts everyone after they finish.

A teacher **learns** from his students.

Maya tells Mr. Dexter about medieval weapons.

"A longbow is for shooting far away. A crossbow is for close-up," says Maya.

A teacher
is **proud** of
his student's
accomplishments.

Joey taught his cousin, Ashley, how to float.

Joey shouts, "Look, Ashley, no hands! You're floating!"

A teacher is a person who . . .

shares what
she knows

explains clearly

coaches

answers questions

finds answers

demonstrates

uses all kinds of
materials

is patient

and encouraging

never gives up

makes learning fun

learns from
students

and is
proud of
his
students.

That's
what a
teacher
is!

About the **Author** and **Photographer**

Barbara Lehn has been involved in regular and special education for more than 25 years. She currently teaches first grade in Concord, Massachusetts, where she continually learns from her students. Barbara lives in Andover, Massachusetts, with her husband and their son.

Carol Krauss turned to professional photography after a career in management consulting. **What Is a Teacher?** is her second collaboration with her friend Barbara Lehn. Carol lives with her family in California and works out of her studio in Massachusetts.